Muscles

Christine Dugan

Consultant

Gina Montefusco, RN
Children's Hospital Los Angeles
Los Angeles, California

Publishing Credits

Dona Herweck Rice, *Editor-in-Chief*; Lee Aucoin, *Creative Director*; Don Tran, *Print Production Manager*; Timothy J. Bradley, *Illustration Manager*; Chris McIntyre, *Editorial Director*; James Anderson, *Associate Editor*; Jamey Acosta, *Associate Editor*; Neri Garcia, *Senior Designer*; Peter Balaskas, *Editorial Administrator*; Stephanie Reid, *Photo Editor*; Jane Gould, *Editor*; Rachelle Cracchiolo, M.S.Ed., *Publisher*

Image Credits

cover Sadeugra/cloki/Shutterstock; p.1 Sadeugra/cloki/Shutterstock; p.4 (left) Jaren Jai Wicklund/Dreamstime,(right) Godfer| Dreamstime; p.5 Rick Nease/Image Source; p.6 Rick Nease; p.7 (top left) Graffizone/iStockphoto, (top center) Hongqi Zhang/Dreamstime.(top right) Salma001/Dreamstime, (bottom) Linda Bucklin/iStockphoto; p.8 (background) UltraOrto, S.A./Shutterstock , Monkey Business Images/Shutterstock (foreground); p.9 (top) hkannn/Shutterstock, (bottom) Douglas R Hess/Shutterstock; p.10 Stephanie Reid; p.11 (left) Rick Nease, (bottom) Stephanie Reid; p.12 Sean Locke/iStockphoto; p.13 Willie B.Thomas/iStockphoto; p.14 paulaphoto/Shutterstock; p.15 Blamb/Shutterstock; p.16 iofoto/Shutterstock; p.17 (top) Paul Matthew Photography/Shutterstock, (bottom) Linda Bucklin/Shutterstock; p.18 Linda Bucklin/Shutterstock; p.19 Sebike/Dreamstime; p.20 Linda Bucklin/Shutterstock; p.21 Ciska76/Dreamstime; p.22 Muellek Josef/Shutterstock; p.23 (left) Josh Hodge/iStockphoto, (bottom) Sonya Etchison/Shutterstock; p.24 Kristian Sekulic/Shutterstock; p.25 Christopher Futcher/Shutterstock; p.26 (top) Christopher Futcher/Shutterstock, (bottom) Inga Nielsen/Shutterstock; p.27 Max Delson Martins Santos/Shutterstock; p.28 Rocket400 Studio/Shutterstock; p.29 Ana Clark; p.32 Dr.James Andrews

Teacher Created Materials

5301 Oceanus Drive
Huntington Beach, CA 92649-1030
http://www.tcmpub.com
ISBN 978-1-4333-1433-9
©2011 Teacher Created Materials, Inc.
Reprinted 2013

Table of Contents

All About Muscles

How do you walk or jump? You use muscles (muhs-uhls)! Muscles let you move. But did you know that they also work when you are still?

Muscles help to give your body its shape. There are more than 600 muscles in your body!

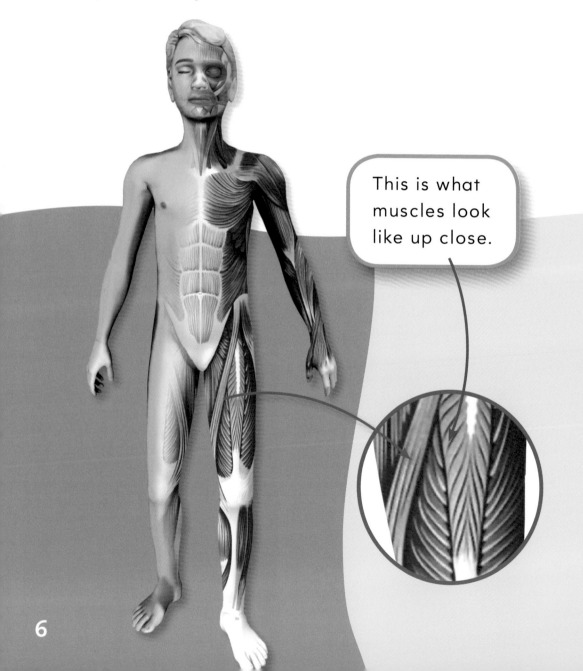

This is what muscles look like up close.

You have over 30 muscles in your face alone. They help you make all kinds of faces, like angry, sad, and happy. Try it!

Say It!

It takes 72 muscles to speak just one word.

Muscles are like rubber bands. The stretchy bands are made of long cells. The cells are called **fibers**. Thousands of tiny fibers are in each muscle.

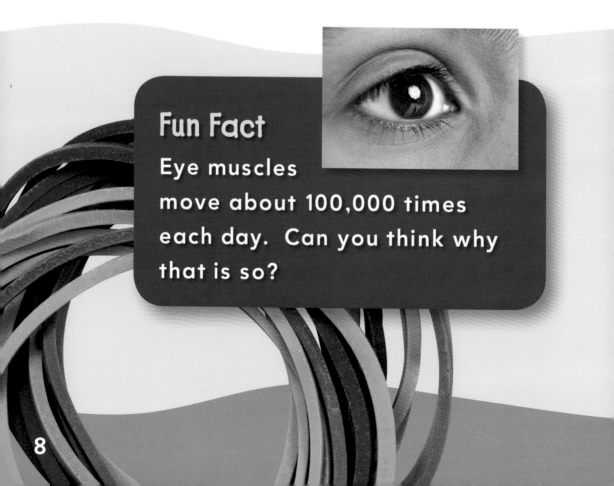

Fun Fact

Eye muscles move about 100,000 times each day. Can you think why that is so?

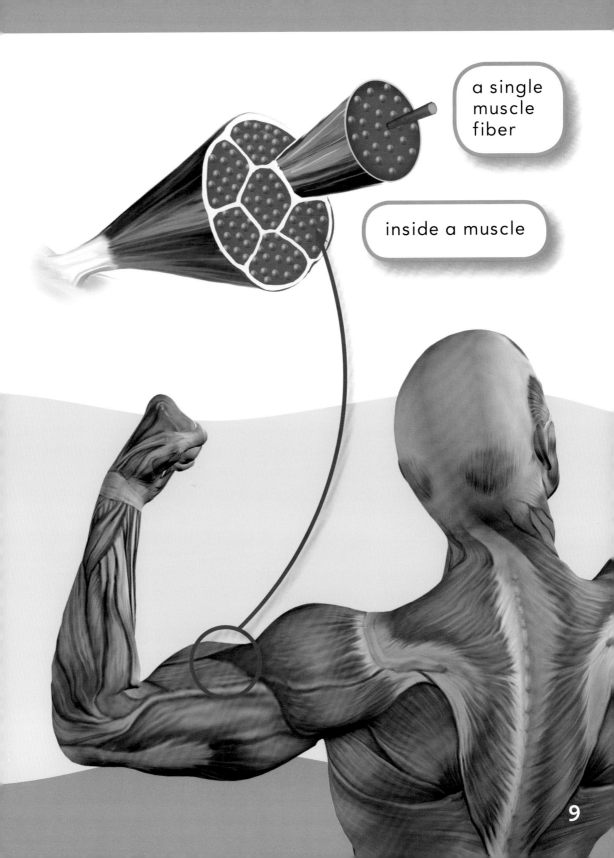

Types of Muscles

There are three kinds of muscles. They are called **skeletal** (SKEL-i-tl), smooth, and **cardiac** (KAHR-dee-ak) muscles. Each of these types of muscles do different things.

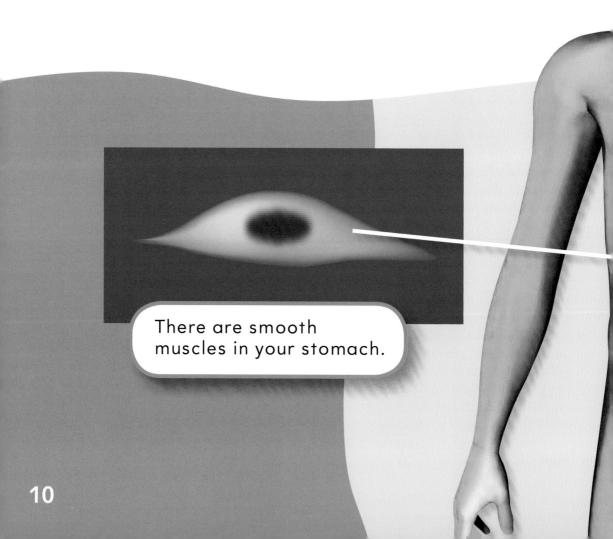

There are smooth muscles in your stomach.

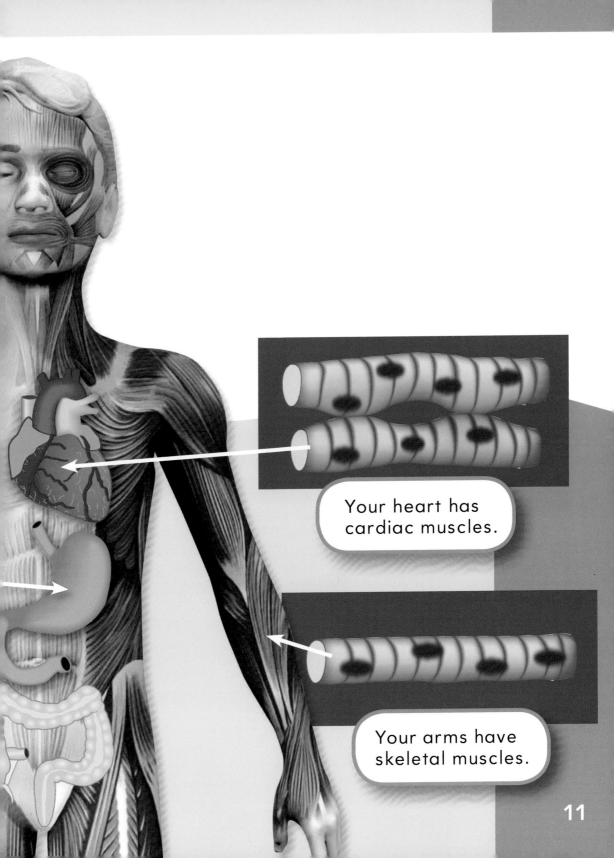

Your heart has cardiac muscles.

Your arms have skeletal muscles.

Smooth muscles do things that you do not have to think about. They just work on their own.

Smooth muscles are in the stomach, intestines, and bladder.

For example, the muscles in your stomach know what to do with food. The muscles just do their job.

Cardiac muscles also work on their own. They are found in your heart. These muscles keep your heart beating. You do not need to tell them what to do.

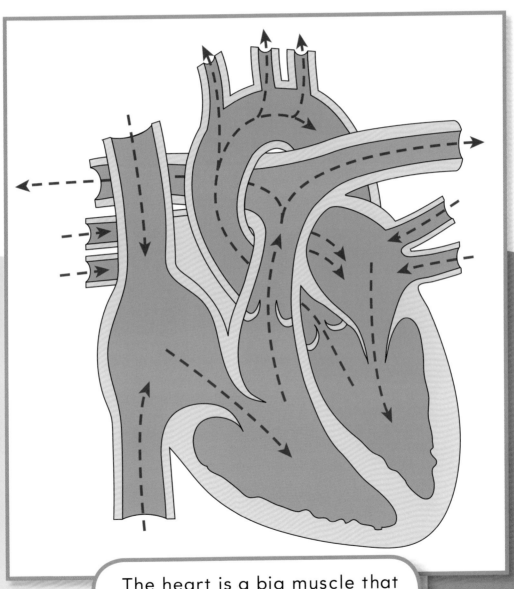

The heart is a big muscle that keeps your blood moving.

You can control some muscles. How do you write? You use a pencil and move your hand. Your brain tells these skeletal muscles to move.

Fun Fact

It is easier to smile than to frown. Frowning uses more muscles than smiling!

There are about 17 muscles that make your fingers and hand work.

Skeletal muscles are attached to bones.
They help you move.

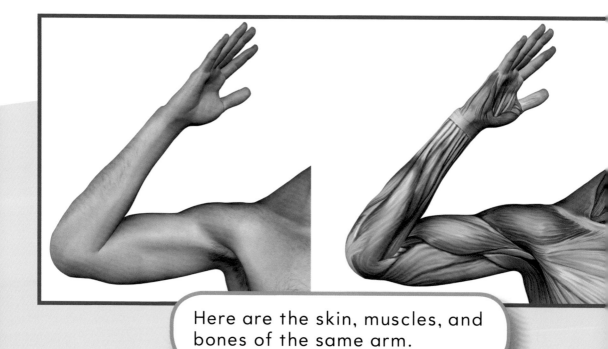

Here are the skin, muscles, and
bones of the same arm.

Muscles are on each side of a bone **joint**. Muscles stretch and shrink as joints bend.

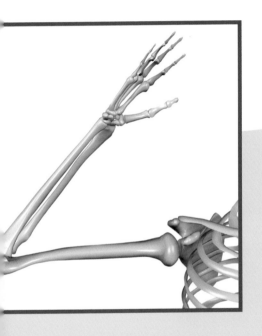

Muscles and joints work together so you can move.

Muscles are attached to bones
by **tendons**.

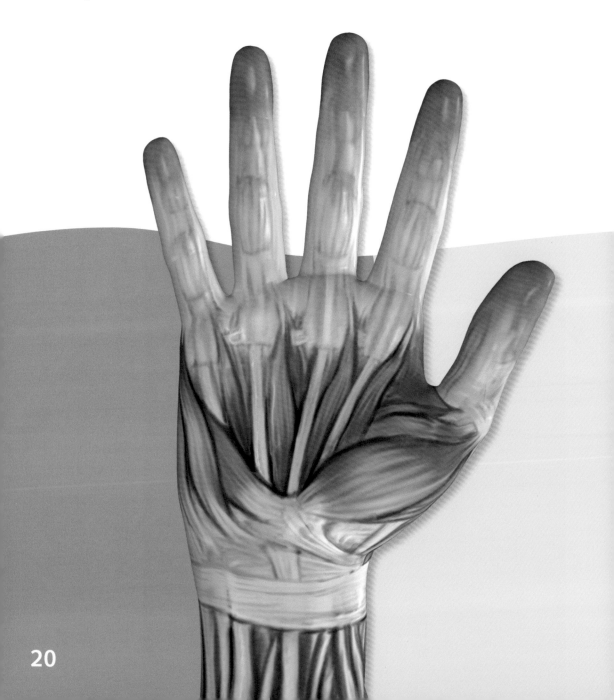

The longest and strongest tendon is in your heel. It is called your Achilles (uh-KIL-eez) tendon.

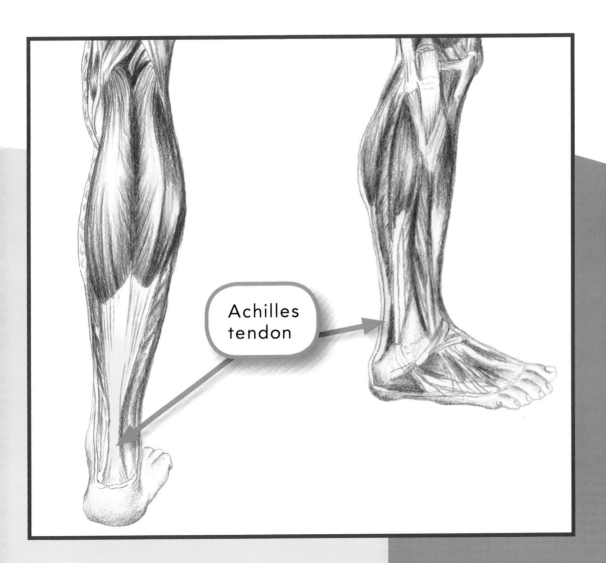

Take Care of Your Muscles

Exercise is good for your muscles. They grow stronger when you use them.

Muscles also grow bigger as they grow stronger.

Take care of your muscles. Stretch them every day. Be careful not to pull a muscle! This means that your muscle tears. Then it must heal.

Your muscles help you do many things. They work even when you are not thinking about them. Exercise and eat healthy foods. Stay healthy so that your muscles do, too!

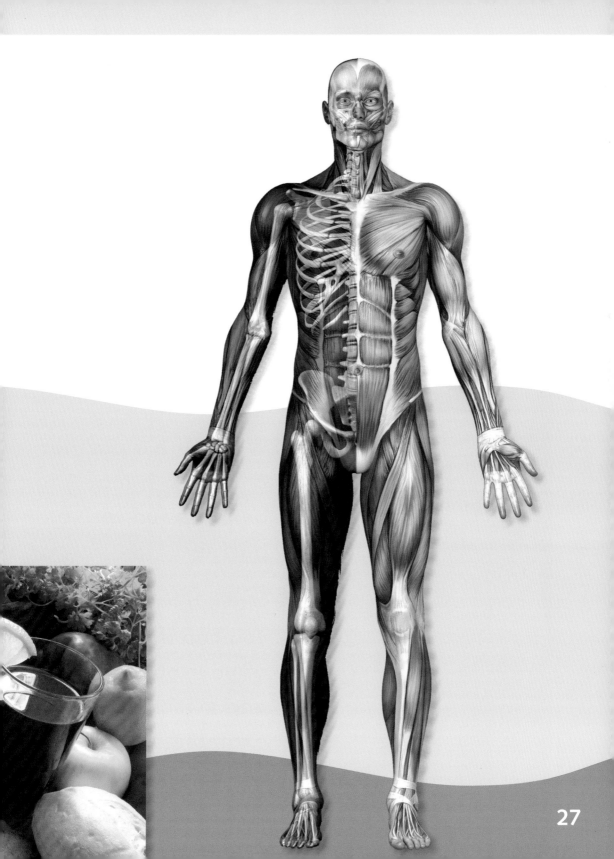

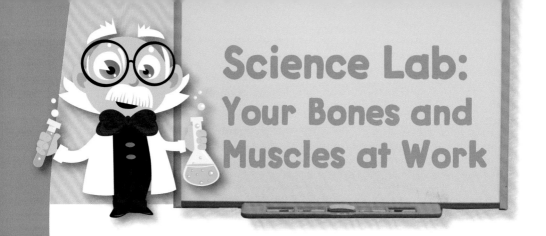

Science Lab: Your Bones and Muscles at Work

What can your body do thanks to your bones and muscles? Find out.

Materials:

- pencils and crayons
- paper

Procedure:

1 Work with a partner or alone. It may be more fun with a partner!

2 Make a list of things you can do because of your bones and muscles. For example, you can write, run, and jump.

3 Choose 5 things from your list and do them.

4 Draw pictures of you and your partner doing the things from your list.

5 Draw arrows to show which muscles and bones you use when you do those activities.

Glossary

cardiac—related to the heart

fibers—cells in the muscles

joint—the place where two bones come together

skeletal—related to the skeleton, or bones of the body

tendon—a tough band of tissue that links a muscle to some other part, like a bone

Index

A Scientist Today

Top athletes depend on Dr. James Andrews! He has helped famous athletes, such as Drew Brees and Michael Jordan, keep their muscles healthy and strong. He is best known for his surgeries on the shoulders, knees, and elbows of Major League Baseball and National Football League stars.